I LEARN ABOUT THE GIFTS OF THE HOLY SPIRIT

WRITTEN BY MARIE CHAPIAN

ILLUSTRATED BY PETER CHAPIAN

Creation House
Carol Stream, Illinois

Printed in the United States of America.

ISBN 0-88419-099-4
Library of Congress Catalog Card Number 74-18151

To CHRISTA and LIZA,
GOD'S most precious
gifts to us

When I receive gifts, usually it's because of a holiday - my birthday or else Christmas!

But God gives us gifts every day — not just
on special occasions.

His most wonderful gifts to me are His Son
and His Holy Spirit.

The Lord Jesus Christ lives in my heart because
I asked Him to be my Savior.

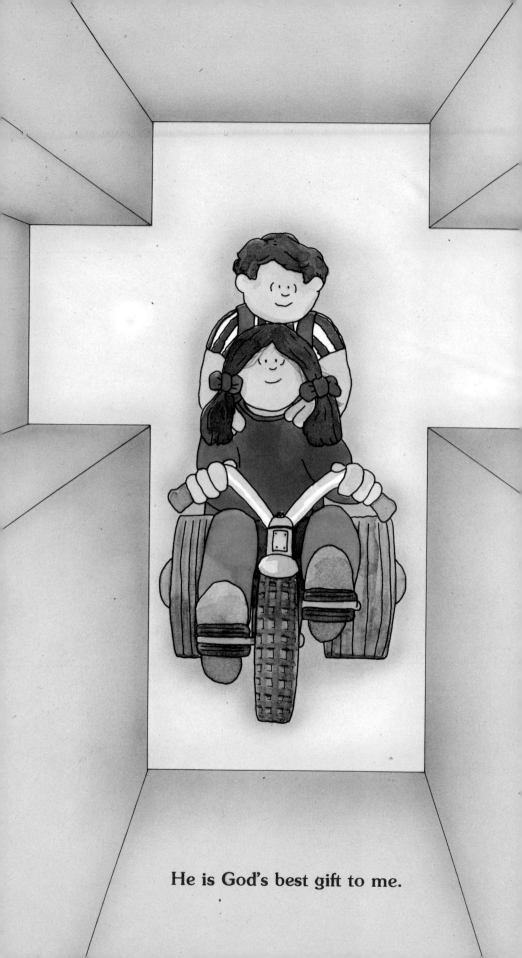

He is God's best gift to me.

I asked Jesus to baptize me with the Holy Spirit,
and Jesus answered my prayer.

ST. LUKE 11

11 If a son shall ask bread of any of you that is a father, will he give him a stone? or if *he* ask a fish, will he for a fish give him a serpent?

12 Or if he shall ask an egg, will he offer him a scorpion?

13 If ye then, being evil, know how to give good gifts unto your children: how much more shall *your* heavenly Father give the Holy Spirit to them that ask him?

14 And he was castin devil, and it was dum came to pass, when was gone out, the du and the people wond

15 But some He casteth out Be-el'-ze-bub devils.

16 And otl sought of h heaven.

I am baptized with the Holy Spirit now and I am sure of it. Jesus promises in the Bible that He will always give His Spirit when we ask.

Even though I am a child, I want to receive God's gifts to me through the Holy Spirit.

The gifts of the Holy Spirit are wonderful blessings that God gives to His children to help make us stronger and happier and better able to fight against the enemy, the Devil.

Here are some of the gifts of the Holy Spirit
that God gives:

THE WORD OF WISDOM

The Holy Spirit sometimes makes me understand many things. It is not what I see with my eyes but what I know in my heart. This wisdom is not just me being smart — it comes from God. When I speak God's words of wisdom, people are helped, and they know that Jesus is real.

**The Gift of Wisdom also helps me
understand what I read in the Bible.**

THE WORD OF KNOWLEDGE

The Holy Spirit sometimes tells me facts that I wouldn't know any other way. This helps other people understand that God knows everything. The gifts of knowledge and wisdom go together. The wisdom of God helps me to kno what to do with the knowledge God gives me.

The Holy Spirit teaches me that ordinary knowledge will someday be useless. But the Lord's knowledge is permanent and will last forever. I can know and understand many things because the Holy Spirit shows me.

THE GIFT OF FAITH

The Holy Spirit helps me to believe in the Lord Jesus
and in every one of His wonderful promises to me.
I know "all things are possible to him who believes."

THE GIFTS OF HEALING

When I am sick, I ask the Lord Jesus to make me well, and He answers my prayer.

I ask the Lord to heal others, too, and He answers my prayers and they get well. The Bible says Jesus wants us to be healed and healthy.

THE EFFECTING OF MIRACLES

Miracles really do happen! A miracle is something that is impossible for a person to do, but with God nothing is impossible. I can ask the Lord to do a miracle, and if He agrees that I need it, it will happen.

THE GIFT OF PROPHECY
The Lord Jesus speaks through people with His very own words to make the church stronger and better. I want Him to use me to speak His words to the people, too.

THE GIFT OF DISCERNING OF SPIRITS
I can know what is right and wrong, and what is from the Spirit of God or from the Devil.

I can speak in a language that I have never heard before.
It is a heavenly language that the Holy Spirit gives me.
God uses it to give a message to everyone in church.
It has to be followed by the same thing in English so we al
understand what God said to us.

THE INTERPRETATION OF TONGUES
I can tell what the Holy Spirit is saying when I
hear a heavenly language spoken. I open my
mouth and tell others.

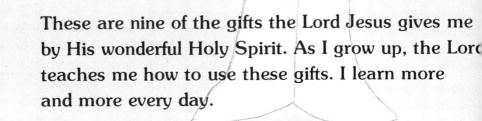

These are nine of the gifts the Lord Jesus gives me by His wonderful Holy Spirit. As I grow up, the Lord teaches me how to use these gifts. I learn more and more every day.

Jesus gives us these wonderful gifts of the Holy Spirit so we can help each other and so Christians will be strong and wise and good.

The Lord Jesus wants us to have power. He does no
want us to be weak. That is why He gives us His
Holy Spirit and the wonderful gifts of the Holy Spiri

Thank You, Lord Jesus, for teaching me about Your wonderful gifts.

Thank You, Lord Jesus, for my wonderful Holy Spirit.